LET'S GO
FISHING
IN THE OCEAN

GEORGE TRAVIS

The Rourke Corporation, Inc.
Vero Beach, Florida 32964

PHOTO CREDITS
© Chad Ehlers/International Stock: cover; ©Kirk Anderson/International Stock: page 15; © Kadir Kir/International Stock: page 16; © East Coast Studios: pages 9, 18; © Corel: pages 4, 6, 7, 10, 12, 13, 19

FISH ILLUSTRATIONS: © Duane Raver

PROJECT EDITOR: Duane Raver
Duane Raver received a degree in Zoology with a major in fishery management from Iowa State University. Employed by the North Carolina Wildlife Resources Commission as a fishery biologist in 1950, he transferred to the Education Division in 1960. He wrote and illustrated for the magazine *Wildlife in North Carolina*. Mr. Raver retired as the editor in 1979 and is a freelance writer and illustrator.

EDITORIAL SERVICES: Penworthy Learning Systems

Library of Congress Cataloging-in-Publication Data

Travis, George. 1961-
   Let's go fishing in the ocean / by George Travis.
      p. cm. — (Let's go fishing)
   Includes index
   Summary: Describes some of the methods used to catch fish that live in the ocean.
   ISBN 0-86593-463-0
   1. Saltwater fishing—Juvenile literature. [1. Saltwater fishing.
2. Fishing.] I. Title. II. Series: Travis, George, 1961-
Let's go fishing.
SH457.T735 1998
799.1'6—dc21   97–49076
                                                            CIP
                                                            AC

Printed in the USA

TABLE OF CONTENTS

FISHING IN THE OCEAN

Most ocean fishing is done from boats. Deeper water often holds more kinds of fish.

The ocean has **habitats** (HAB eh TATS) for different kinds of fish. Some fish like to live around sandbanks. Other kinds of fish like reefs because they have many places to hide from **predators** (PRED uh turz). Shipwrecks are good habitats for these fish, too.

Casting (KAST ing) a line from the beach into the ocean, or surf, is called surfcasting. Surfcasting is a great way to catch fish without going out in a boat.

This sea plant makes a great hiding place for this grouper.

BIG FISH, LITTLE FISH

The ocean is home to thousands of different kinds of fish. Some are tiny—the size of your thumb. Others, like the whale shark, can grow to 50 feet long (15 meters)—as wide as a basketball court!

People catch many different size fish, like this large Nassau grouper.

Marlins are one of the largest game fish found in the ocean.

Fishing in the ocean, or saltwater fishing, can be hard work! Many fish in the ocean are big, fast, and strong. Some of the fastest and strongest are the marlin, sailfish, swordfish, and tuna. The barracuda and tarpon are smaller, but they can put up a long, hard fight.

SURFCASTING

The rods used for surfcasting are usually longer than other rods. The reels are larger, too. The rods are made to reach from the shore to where the fish are feeding.

Most people use a rod rest or sand spike after casting their line. This way they don't have to hold the rod while waiting for fish to bite. You can buy rod rests, but a plastic tube from a hardware store works just as well.

Choose your **bait** (BAYT) to match the type of fish you want to catch. You can use **artificial lures** (AHR tuh FUSH ul LOORZ) or natural bait, like blood worms, crabs, shrimp, and small fish.

These men have set up their rod rests ready for a day of surfcasting.

GOING FOR THE BIG ONE

Fishing from a moving boat is called trolling. Trolling is used to catch big game fish like marlin or tuna. The moving bait looks like the living food these fish eat.

Most troll boats have four fishing rods—two on the back and one on each side. The rods on the sides have their lines held by arms, called outriggers. Outriggers keep the fishing line away from the sides of the boat.

The bait closest to the boat often catches the most fish. This may be because some fish like the **wake** (WAYK), the track the boat makes in the water.

Fish seem to like the wake of a boat.

HOW TO CATCH A SHARK

    Drift fishing is a great way to catch a shark. Take a boat to a place where sharks are known to be. Turn the engine off and let the boat drift.

    Then fill a mesh bag with **chum** (CHUM). Chum is tiny pieces of fish and fish oil or blood. Hang the bag of chum over the edge of the boat.

These fishermen have just caught a small shark.

Sharks, like this large silky shark, have a very strong sense of smell.

As the boat moves, tiny pieces of chum go through the mesh and make a trail in the ocean. The trail is called a "smell-lane." A hungry shark may smell the trail and follow it—to one of the fishing lines on your boat!

CHARTERING A BOAT

Some people like to charter a boat when they want to fish at sea. Chartering means they pay to ride on a boat with a captain to drive it. The boat has all the fishing gear and bait they will need. Sometimes the captain or the mate will give a fishing lesson, too.

Charter boats are used for game fishing. They have outriggers for trolling and chairs for fighting large, heavy fish, like marlin or tuna.

These kids use a small fishing boat to reach deeper water.

BIG OCEAN BAIT

Using the right bait is important. Bait has to look or smell like the fish's natural food to fool the fish into biting on the hook.

Most artificial, or man-made, lures look like a fish in the water—though they don't look like a fish out of the water. For bottom-feeding fish, use a lure that looks like a shrimp.

Shellfish, crabs, eels, and cut fish are natural bait. The fresher the fish, the better it will stay on your hook. Whole fish or whole squid is good bait for catching large fish. Most of the time live bait works better than dead bait.

An angler used a large artificial squid to lure this fish.

REELING IT IN

When a fish has taken the bait, and the hook is set firmly in its mouth, you need to tire it out so that you can reel it in safely.

After you hook a fish, let it swim as far as it wants to.

This boy waits patiently for a fish to strike his bait.

Gaffs are used to haul very large fish, like this tuna, into the boat.

Later, when the fish slows and turns around, wind in as much line as you can.

Next, bring your rod up to pull the fish toward you. Then quickly lower the rod and wind in any slack line. Repeat these steps until the fish is close enough for you to pull it in with a net or **gaff** (GAF), a large steel hook.

SAFETY

Remember to take sunblock and a long-sleeved shirt if you are surf fishing or going out on a boat. Sunglasses will protect your eyes from the sun and the glare off the water.

If you are going on a charter boat, wear a life jacket and listen to the captain's safety advice.

When you leave the beach after fishing, think about the wildlife and other people who use the beach. Take old line, hooks, and trash with you.

fish: Atlantic sailfish *(Istiophorus platypterus)*
average weight: 75 to 100 lbs.
(34 to 45.4 kilograms), may reach
128 lbs. (58 kilograms)
location: Atlantic ocean

---

fish: blue marlin *(Makaira nigricans)*
average weight: 275 to 400 (124.7
to 181.4 kilograms), may
reach 2,000 lbs. (907 kilograms)
location: worldwide

---

fish: dolphinfish *(Coryphaena hippurus)*
average weight: 25 to 40 lbs.
(11.3 to 18 kilograms), may
reach 88 lbs. (40 kilograms)
location: worldwide in
tropical and warm-temperature seas

---

fish: blackfin tuna *(Thunnus atlanticus)*
average weight: less than 10 lbs.
(4.5 kilograms), may reach
42 lbs. (19 kilograms)
location: Atlantic from
Massachusetts to Brazil

fish: great barracuda *(Sphyraena barracuda)*
average weight: 25 to 35 lbs.
(11.3 to 15.9 kilograms),
may reach 106 lbs.
(48 kilograms)
location: tropical and warm temperature Atlantic waters, and the Mediterranean and Black Seas

---

fish: scalloped hammerhead *(Sphyrna lewini)*
average weight: 300 to 400 lbs.
(136 to 181.4 kilograms)
location: tropical waters
in both the Atlantic and
eastern Pacific

---

fish: tarpon *(Megalops atlanticus)*
average weight: 20 to 80 lbs.
(9.1 and 36.3 kilograms), may
reach 300 lbs. (136 kilograms)
location: western Atlantic, Gulf of Mexico, the
Carribean, west coast of Central America, and coast of
northwest Africa

---

fish: yellowfin grouper *(Mycteroperca venenosa)*
average weight: 20 lbs. (9.1 kilograms)
location: Bermuda and Florida
to Brazil

GLOSSARY

artificial (AHR tuh FISH ul) — made by human beings rather than nature

bait (BAYT) — something, usually food, placed on a hook to attract fish

casting (KAST ing) — method of throwing the line with bait into the water

chum (CHUM) — tiny pieces of fish and fish oil or blood

gaff (GAF) — large iron hook used to pull large fish onto a boat or onto shore

habitats (HAB eh TATS) — places where animals or plants live and grow naturally

lure (LOOR) — man-made bait used to attract and catch fish

predators (PRED uh turz) — animals that eat other animals

wake (WAYK) — track or path a moving boat or ship makes in the water

INDEX

FURTHER READING:

Find out more about fishing with these helpful books and information sites:
The Dorling Kindersley Encyclopedia of Fishing. The Complete Guide to the Fish, Tackle, & Techniquies of Fresh & Saltwater Angling. Dorling Kindersley, Inc., 1994
Griffen, Steven A., *The Fishing Sourcebook: Your One-Stop Resource for Everything You Need to Feed Your Fishing Habit.* The Globe Pequot Press, 1996
Price, Steven D. *The Ultimate Fishing Guide.* HarperCollins, 1996
Fishernet online at www.thefishernet.com
National Marine Fisheries Service online at www.nmfs.gov
World of Fishing online at www.fishingworld.com